ISBN-13: 9798393547325

Cover design by: Wendell S. Jr.
Library of Congress Control Number: 2018675309
Printed in the United States of America

HIP HOP MOTIVATION:THE BUSINESS OF MUSIC

Wendell Saxton Jr.

Budding Potential

CONTENTS

CHAPTER 1

Introduction to the Music Industry Landscape

The music industry is a complex network of various players and elements that work together in order to create, produce and distribute music. In this chapter, we will introduce you to the different components of the music industry and how they interact with each other. We will also explore the various revenue streams and income sources for music artists, as well as the legal and administrative aspects of the music industry.

Section 1: The Different Players in the Music Industry

The music industry is made up of a variety of players, each with a specific role to play in the development and dissemination of music. Here are some of the key players:

1. Record Labels - Record labels are major players in the music business. They are responsible for discovering and signing new talent, managing the production and distribution of recorded music, and promoting and marketing the artists and music. Labels have in-house teams who handle everything from packaging and design, to promotion and distribution.

2. Music Publishers - Music publishers manage the ownership and licensing of music copyrights. They ensure that the artist's music is published and administered correctly, allowing them to collect royalties from their works. Publishers also help with licensing, copyright extensions and research, and document and commercial printing.

3. Artist Managers - Artist managers represent the artist and oversee all aspects of their career. They negotiate deals, manage day-to-day tasks, oversee finances, and ensure the artist is moving in the right direction. They help to create a strategic plan based on the artist's vision, goals and music style, and ensure that the artist is properly protected legally when signing deals.

4. Agents - Agents act as intermediaries between the artist and promoters\\\/venues. Their role is to negotiate deals, book gigs, manage the artist's schedule, and manage logistics. Their role is vital to making sure that the artist spends time on stage, working on their craft, and promoting their brand.

5. Promoters - Promoters are responsible for producing and promoting live events. They work with agents to book artists for live shows, advertise and market the event, and manage logistics. They ensure that the live shows and tours are profitable and within schedule, while also making sure the artist is provided with everything they need to perform at their best.

Section 2: Identifying Revenue Streams for Music Artists

A music artist's income can come from several sources, including album sales, streaming royalties, merchandise sales, live performances, brand endorsements, and sync licensing. However, revenue streams can vary depending on the artist's level of success, genre, and distribution method.

For example, established artists may generate more revenue from live shows and merchandise sales, while emerging artists may rely on streaming royalties and sync licensing for their income.

Music artists can create revenues from multiple sources, including:

1. Record Sales - Artists earn money from sales of their music, both physical and digital. Record sales are mostly generated through streaming platforms and record stores, retailers and distribution outlets.

2. Streaming Royalties - Streaming platforms such as Spotify and Apple Music provide a source of revenue for artists whenever their music is played. Streaming is a key part of the music industry, and artists get paid per stream

from streaming platforms, which helps improve their earnings over time.

3. Live Shows - Artists get paid for live performances at events and concerts. Live shows are a significant revenue source for artists, and the money they earn from them can help keep their career afloat, especially during downtimes between album releases and other projects.

4. Merchandise - Selling merchandise like t-shirts, posters, and albums can be an additional source of revenue. Fans love to buy merchandise to support the artists they love and feel they have a personal connection with. Selling merchandise can help an artist generate extra income and maintain control of their brand.

5. Sync Licensing - Artists can earn money

by licensing their music for use in films, television shows, commercials and other types of media. Sync licensing is one of the most important aspects of the music industry, and it can help an artist reach new audiences and gain exposure for their work.

Section 3: Legal and Administrative Aspects of the Music Industry

Legal and administrative aspects of the music industry are crucial for music artists to understand. For example, an artist must understand copyright law and how to protect their intellectual property rights. Additionally, music artists need to comprehend music contracts and the services provided by music labels, distributors, and publishing companies.

Musicians should also be aware of administrative tasks such as taxes, accounting, and booking agents.

The music industry has a variety of legal and administrative components that impact artists and their careers. These include:

1. Copyright Law - Artists must legally protect their music and associated content. Copyright law ensures that they are adequately compensated for the use of their intellectual property. This includes revenue generated from streaming platforms, live performances, merchandise sales, and other sources.

2. Recording Contracts - Record labels and artists sign contracts outlining the terms under which the label will produce and

distribute the artist's music. These contracts dictate the terms of the deal, such as royalties, album rights, and creative control.

3. Distribution Agreements - Distribution agreements give the right to distribute physical and digital recordings of music in specific territories. They specify the distribution channels and the dates the music will be released.

4. Management Agreements - These agreements outline the relationship between the artist and their manager, including fee arrangements, commission structure, and the scope of work. Management agreements also cover concert promotion, music production, and marketing deals.

The music industry is a complex network of various players and elements that work together to create and distribute music. Understanding the different components, revenue streams, and legal/administrative structures is crucial for aspiring artists who want to succeed in this business. In the next chapter, we will dive deeper into the concept of royalties and how artists can maximize their earnings.

Understanding the music industry landscape is fundamental for success as a music artist. By exploring the different players and revenue streams available, music artists can make informed decisions about their career and maximise their income. Moreover, having a grasp of legal and administrative aspects will ensure that artists protect their rights and avoid legal troubles. In the next chapters, we will dive deeper into each aspect of the music industry landscape to provide a more comprehensive understanding of the industry.

CHAPTER 2

*Building Your Brand
and Marketing Yourself
as an Artist*

Building a brand and marketing yourself as a hip hop artist is a crucial step in establishing your presence in the music industry. It involves creating a unique brand identity, using social media and other digital tools to market your music, and building a fan base.

Building your brand and marketing yourself effectively is crucial if you want to succeed in the music industry. In this chapter, we will explore how to create a unique brand identity, how to use social media and other digital tools to promote your music, and how to build a fanbase and engage with your audience.

Section 1: Creating a Unique Brand Identity as a Hip Hop Artist

As a hip hop artist, it's essential to create a unique brand identity that reflects your style, values, and personality. This identity can be reflected in your stage name, your music, your fashion style, and your overall image. Developing a memorable brand identity can help you stand out in a crowded industry, making it easier for fans, record labels, and music industry professionals to identify and remember you.

When creating a unique brand identity as a hip hop artist, there are four key factors you need to consider:

1. Choose a Unique Stage Name - Your stage name is your first point of contact

with your audience. Make it easy to spell, memorable, and unique. Consider using your real name, a nickname, or an alter ego that represents your unique style and personality.

2. Develop Your Image - Your image is how your fans identify you. Create a consistent image across all your social media platforms, videos, and press photos. This can include clothing, jewelry, hairstyles, tattoos, or makeup that reflects your personal style and brand identity.

3. Define Your Music Style - Define your music style to create a unique sound that helps distinguish you as an artist. Experiment with different instruments, beats, and lyrics until you find a sound that sets you apart from other artists.

4. Collaborate with Other Artists - Collaborating with other artists can help you create new sounds, fanbases, and broaden your reach. Find complementary artists who share your vision and style to create a unique and diverse roster.

Section 2: Utilizing Social Media and Other Digital Tools to Market Your Music

Social media platforms such as Instagram, Twitter, and TikTok offer artists powerful tools to expand their reach and connect with fans worldwide. Artists can use these platforms to share their music, engage with fans, and provide behind-the-scenes glimpses into their lives. Other digital tools such as YouTube, Spotify, and Apple Music provide additional opportunities for artists to get discovered, build their audience, and monetize their music.

When using social media and other digital tools, it's important to maintain consistency in your branding, post content regularly, and engage with your fanbase regularly. Creating a content calendar can help you plan out your social media strategy and ensure that you remain consistent with your messaging.

Here are some ways to effectively use social media and other digital tools to market your music and build a loyal fanbase:

1. Post Regular Content - Keep your fans engaged with regular content, including videos, photos, and behind-the-scenes glimpses of your life as a musician. Share your thoughts about current events, politics, or personal issues that affect you

or your music.

2. Engage with Your Audience - Respond to comments, DMs, and messages as often as you can. Ask for feedback and inspire fan collaboration on your music. Take the time to acknowledge your fans personally, especially if they've supported you from the beginning.

3. Utilize Ads - Utilize social media ads and redirects to increase awareness and visibility of your brand and music. Be sure to tailor them to your target audience, including demographics, location, and interests.

4. Create a Website - Create a professional website to house all of your information, music, videos, and tour dates in one place. Make it easy to navigate, mobile-friendly,

and visually appealing. Remember to include calls-to-action and sign-up forms to build your email list.

Section 3: Building a Fanbase and Engaging with Your Audience

Building a fanbase requires hard work, dedication, and patience. It involves connecting with your audience, both online and offline, and providing value beyond your music. Fans want to feel like they have a personal connection with the artists they enjoy, and as an artist, it's your job to cultivate that connection.

Engaging with your fans can take many forms, such as responding to messages and comments, holding meet-and-greets, and performing live shows. You can also create exclusive content for your fans, such as behind-the-scenes videos or merchandise.

Building a fanbase and engaging with your audience is essential to the longevity of your career as a hip hop artist. Here are some ways to create a loyal fanbase and connect with your audience:

1. Engage with Fans at Live Shows - Make your fans feel special by engaging with them at live events. Go out of your way to connect with them, whether through performing dedicated song verses or simply interacting with them during the show. This will create lasting memories and build a dedicated fanbase.

2. Create Unique Merchandise - Create unique and official merchandise to help bridge the gap between you and your fans.

Fans don't only want physical merchandise but a physical representation of their experience with you. Consider designing merchandise with your image or logos, including t-shirts, hats, posters, or stickers.

3. Host Special Events - Connect with your audience by hosting special events such as secret shows, meet-and-greets, and listening parties. This is a great way to foster a stronger sense of community and build closer relationships with your fans. Share exclusive content and merchandise during these events to create a memorable experience.

4. Collaborate with Your Fans - Allow for fan collaboration, whether it's on music or artwork, as a way to involve them in the creative process and recognize their influence in the making of your music.

Share fan-generated content on your social media platforms and website to acknowledge and celebrate their contributions.

Creating and promoting a unique brand identity as a hip hop artist is crucial to your success in the music industry. By focusing on developing each section, you can establish yourself as an influential and respected artist in your genre. Remember to remain authentic and true to your unique style and personality throughout your career. Engaging with your audience will be the backbone of your fanbase, so make sure to respond to them with sincerity and appreciation.

CHAPTER 3

Navigating Contracts and Negotiating Deals

As a hip hop artist, it is essential to understand the common contracts and agreements in the music industry, how to negotiate for better terms and conditions, and how to protect your rights and maintain ownership of your work. In this chapter, we will explore all of these topics to help you navigate contracts and negotiate deals with confidence.

Navigating contracts and negotiating deals is a critical step for any music artist seeking to advance their career. It involves understanding typical contracts and agreements in the music industry, negotiating for better terms and conditions, and protecting your rights and maintaining ownership of your work.

Section 1: Understanding Common Contracts and Agreements in the Music Industry

Music industry contracts can range from recording deals, distribution agreements, publishing contracts, to licensing agreements. Understanding the terms and conditions of these contracts is essential, as it sets out the legal obligations of both parties and can have long-term financial and creative implications.

Some common terms you may encounter include advances, royalties, recoupment, creative control, and ownership rights. It's essential to consult with a music attorney before entering into any contract or agreement to ensure that you fully understand the terms and conditions outlined.

Before entering into any contracts or agreements, it is important to understand the common types of contracts and agreements in the music industry. Here are some essential contracts and agreements to look out for:

1. Recording Contracts - A recording contract is a legal agreement between an artist and a record label, which gives the label the right to distribute the artist's music. It includes terms for royalty rates, advances, copyright ownership, and length of the contract.

2. Publishing Contracts - A publishing contract is a legal agreement between an artist and a publishing company that gives the publisher the right to license and

administer the artist's music. It also includes terms for royalty rates, advances, copyright ownership, and length of the contract.

3. Management Contracts - A management contract is a legal agreement between an artist and a manager, which outlines the responsibilities and compensation of the manager. It includes terms for commission rates, termination clauses, and length of the contract.

4. Performance Agreements - A performance agreement is a contract between an artist and a promoter or venue that outlines the terms of a live performance, including payment, venue fees, security, and other logistics.

It's important to fully read and understand

any contracts or agreements before signing them. It is also recommended to consult with an attorney or legal expert to ensure you fully understand the terms and language.

Section 2: Negotiating for Better Terms and Conditions

You have the right to negotiate better terms and conditions in your contracts. This can include negotiating for higher advances or royalties, retaining more creative control, or having a say in the ownership rights of your work. It's essential to approach negotiations in a professional and respectful manner to maintain good relationships with your collaborators.

It's important to have a clear

understanding of your brand value and what you bring to the table before entering into negotiations. Be prepared to demonstrate how you can contribute to the success of the project or label you are negotiating with.

Negotiating for better terms and conditions can be a tricky part of the music industry, but it's important to advocate for yourself and your creative work. Here are some tips for negotiating better contracts:

1. Know your worth - Before you begin negotiating, come up with a reasonable estimation of your worth in the industry. This means considering your talent, experience, current market trends, and the value you bring to a project.

2. Be clear about your needs and priorities - Come to the negotiation table with a clear list of priorities to communicate with the other party. This can include anything from providing better promotion, increasing royalty or commission rates, or protecting your intellectual property rights.

3. Remain professional and collaborative - Negotiations should never turn hostile, remain professional and open-minded during the negotiation process. You can communicate your needs and priorities, but avoid being combative or dismissive of the other party's interests.

4. Consider hiring a representative - If you're not comfortable negotiating on your own behalf, consider hiring a representative such as an attorney, manager or agent to help you navigate the

negotiation process.

Section 3: Protecting Your Rights and Maintaining Ownership of Your Work

Protecting your rights and maintaining ownership of your work is crucial. It's important to ensure that you retain ownership of your masters, songwriting, and publishing rights, as these can provide a significant source of income in the long term.

To protect your rights, consider registering your work with the relevant copyright authorities and music industry bodies. Additionally, it's essential to have a clear understanding of any licensing or distribution agreements that you enter into to ensure that you maintain ownership of your work and receive adequate compensation.

As an artist, it is important to protect your rights and maintain ownership of your creative work. Here are some tips to help protect your work:

1. Register your work - Register your music, lyrics, and other creative content with the appropriate copyright office to protect your intellectual property rights.

2. Read contracts carefully - Make sure to read all contracts and agreements carefully to understand the terms and conditions of the contract. If you have any doubts or concerns, contact a legal expert before signing.

3. Retain ownership - Whenever possible, retain ownership of your intellectual

property including your music, lyrics, and other creative works.

4. Negotiate for favorable terms - Negotiate for favorable terms that help protect your rights and give you more control over your creative work.

Navigating contracts and negotiating deals can be intimidating, but with the right knowledge and approach, it can be a beneficial and rewarding process. Understanding common contracts and agreements in the music industry, negotiating for better terms and conditions, and protecting your rights and maintaining ownership of your work are all essential to your success as a hip hop artist in the music industry. Remember to be informed, professional, and collaborative in all of your dealings, and be sure to consult with legal experts when needed. By working with an experienced music attorney, you can ensure that you are making informed decisions that support your career and creative vision.

CHAPTER 4

Building and Managing Your Business Team

As a hip hop artist, you are not just a talented musician, but also a business owner. Building and managing a successful business team is crucial to your success and growth as an artist. In this chapter, we will discuss the important components of building and managing a business team, including finding and hiring the right people for your team, effectively communicating with your team members, and developing your leadership skills.

Section 1: Finding and Hiring the Right People for Your Team

As a music artist, you may require a team of professionals to help manage and promote your career. This may include managers, agents, publicists, lawyers, and accountants. Finding the right people for your team requires careful consideration, research, and due diligence.

When hiring for your team, consider their experience and track record in the music industry, their ability to work collaboratively with other team members, and their understanding of your unique vision and brand identity.

Building a strong and effective team is critical to your success as an artist. Here are some key team members to consider hiring:

1. Manager - A manager is responsible for helping you achieve your goals, managing your schedule, and handling the business aspects of your career, such as negotiating

contracts and securing new opportunities.

2. Agent - An agent is responsible for helping you obtain and book performances, appearances, and other opportunities. They often have existing relationships with industry professionals, such as promoters and booking agents.

3. Lawyer - A lawyer can help protect your legal rights, negotiate contracts, and ensure that your intellectual property is properly protected.

When finding and hiring team members, it's important to look for individuals with experience in the music industry, a strong network of contacts, and a track record of success. You should also consider personality fit and chemistry with your team members, as these relationships will be key to maintaining a cohesive and effective team.

Section 2: Building and Maintaining Effective Communication Within Your Business Team

Communication is key to building and maintaining an effective business team. Establishing clear communication channels, regular meetings and check-ins, and setting clear expectations can help ensure that everyone on your team is aligned towards achieving your goals.

Effective communication also involves being responsive to feedback and being open to constructive criticism. As the leader of your business team, it's essential to create a culture of mutual respect and collaboration, and to foster an environment where everyone feels comfortable sharing their thoughts and ideas.

Effective communication is a fundamental component of any successful business team. Here are some ways to establish and maintain effective communication within your team:

1. Hold regular team meetings - Regular team meetings are an opportunity to build team morale, ensure everyone is informed on developments, receive feedback, and set goals for the future.

2. Use technology to facilitate communication - Utilize various communication technologies such as email, text messages, and video conferencing to ensure that

communication is taking place regularly and effectively.

3. Clearly define roles and expectations - Clearly defining the roles and expectations of each team member will help avoid confusion and miscommunication.

4. Be open and transparent - Open and transparent communication will help build trust with your team members and ensure that everyone is on the same page.

Section 3: Developing Your Leadership Skills as a Hip Hop Artist

As a hip hop artist, you are not just a creative individual; you are also a leader of your team and a role model for your fans. Developing your leadership skills is crucial to building a successful career in the music industry.

Leadership involves setting a clear vision and strategy for your career, making decisions that align with your values and brand identity, and inspiring and motivating others to work towards a common goal.

To develop your leadership skills, you may consider taking courses or workshops, hiring a leadership coach or mentor, or seeking out advice from experienced industry professionals.

Being a successful hip hop artist requires more than just musical talent. Developing your leadership skills is critical to successfully managing your team and growing your career. Here are some ways to develop your leadership skills:

1. Lead by example - Modeling positive behavior and leading by example will help create a positive work culture and earn the respect of your team members.

2. Continuously learn and improve - Continuously learning and improving will help you stay ahead of the curve and set an example for your team members.

3. Be flexible - Being adaptable and flexible is necessary when dealing with the ever-changing nature of the music industry.

4. Set goals and hold yourself accountable - Setting achievable goals and holding yourself accountable will not only help ensure your success but also encourage your team members to do the same.

Building and managing a successful

business team is essential to the success of any hip hop artist. From finding and hiring the right people to maintaining effective communication and developing leadership skills, there are many components involved in building a strong and effective team. With dedication, hard work, and a focus on building strong relationships with your team members, you can achieve success as an artist in the music industry. By finding and hiring the right people for your team, building and maintaining effective communication, and developing your leadership skills, you can create a culture of collaboration, respect, and vision that can help guide your success. Remember that your team is there to support you in achieving your goals, but as the leader, you must also be willing to put in the work and show your commitment to your vision.

CHAPTER 5

Developing a Sustainable Business Strategy

As a hip hop artist, it's important to have a sustainable business strategy that will help you achieve your goals and build a successful career. In this chapter, we will discuss the important components of developing a sustainable business strategy, including setting goals, developing a strategic plan, budgeting and financial management, and identifying opportunities for growth and expansion in the music industry.

Section 1: Setting Goals and Developing a Strategic Plan for Your Music Career

The first step in developing a sustainable business strategy is to set clear goals and develop a strategic plan to achieve those goals. This involves identifying your strengths, weaknesses, opportunities, and threats, and creating a roadmap that outlines your objectives and action steps.

Your strategic plan should include strategies for promoting your music, building your brand, expanding your fan base, and generating revenue. It should also outline your marketing and promotion strategies, tour plans, and collaborations with other artists and industry professionals.

Setting specific and achievable goals is crucial to creating a sustainable business strategy. Here are some key steps to follow:

1. Define your goals - Start by defining what you want to achieve as an artist. This

could include selling a certain number of albums or performing at a certain venue.

2. Make sure your goals are measurable - It's essential to make sure your goals are measurable so that you can track your progress and measure your success.

3. Develop a strategic plan - Once you have set your goals, develop a strategic plan that outlines the steps you need to take to achieve them.

4. Identify your strengths and weaknesses - Be honest about your strengths and weaknesses as an artist and incorporate these into your strategic plan.

Section 2: Budgeting and Financial Management for Music Artists

Managing your finances effectively is a critical component of developing a sustainable business strategy. As a music artist, it's important to have a detailed budget that outlines your expenses and income and helps you make informed decisions about your spending and investments.

You should also establish a system for tracking your income and expenses, including revenue from album sales, royalties, merchandise sales, and touring. This will help you to understand your financial position and make informed decisions about your budget and investments.

Budgeting and financial management are critical aspects of developing a sustainable business strategy. Here are some key steps to follow:

1. Create a budget - Start by creating a budget that covers all of your expenses, including recording costs, touring expenses, and promotional materials.

2. Track your income and expenses - Keep track of your income and expenses to make sure that your budget is accurate.

3. Save money for unexpected expenses - Make sure to save money for unexpected expenses, such as equipment repairs or medical bills.

4. Work with a financial advisor - Consider working with a financial advisor who can help you create a budget and manage your finances more effectively.

Section 3: Identifying Opportunities for Growth and Expansion in the Music Industry

The music industry is constantly evolving, and as a music artist, it's essential to stay up-to-date with the latest trends and opportunities for growth and expansion. This may involve exploring new revenue streams, such as licensing your music for film and television, or partnering with brands for endorsements and sponsorship deals.

It's important to stay connected with other music industry professionals, attend industry events, and engage with your fans to understand their preferences and interests. This will help you to identify new opportunities for growth and expansion, and develop strategies to capitalize on them.

Identifying opportunities for growth and expansion is key to creating a sustainable business strategy. Here are some key steps to follow:

1. Stay informed about industry trends - Stay up-to-date with industry trends and changes that could impact your career.

2. Build relationships with industry professionals - Build relationships with key players in the industry, such as record label executives, producers, and promoters.

3. Be open to new opportunities - Don't be afraid to try new things and explore new opportunities, such as collaborations or partnerships with other artists.

4. Expand your fan base - Focus on expanding your fan base by leveraging social media platforms and engaging with your audience.

Developing a sustainable business strategy is essential to the success of any hip hop artist. By setting specific, measurable goals, developing a strategic plan, budgeting and managing your finances effectively, and identifying opportunities for growth and expansion, you can create a successful career and achieve your dreams in the music industry. Stay informed, be open to new opportunities, and stay focused on your goals, and success will follow. Remember that the music industry is constantly evolving, so it's important to stay informed and flexible, adapt to new trends and changes, and always keep your vision and brand identity at the forefront of your strategy.

CHAPTER 6

Staying Ahead of the Game

As a hip hop artist, it's important to stay ahead of the game to maintain your success and longevity in the music industry. In this chapter, we will discuss the important components of staying ahead of the game, including keeping up with industry trends and changes, building a long-lasting career and legacy as a hip hop artist, and giving back and mentoring the next generation of music artists.

Section 1: Keeping up with Industry Trends and Changes

The music industry is constantly changing, and it's essential to stay informed and adapt to new trends and shifts in the marketplace. This may involve attending industry conferences, networking events, and seminars to learn about new technologies, marketing strategies, and emerging artists.

It's also essential to stay connected with your fans and engage with them through social media, live streams, and local events. This will help you to understand their preferences and interests and create music and content that resonates with them.

Here are some key steps to follow:

1. Stay informed - Keep up with industry news, trends, and emerging technologies through industry publications, blogs, and social media.

2. Attend industry events - Attend industry events such as conferences, trade shows,

and festivals to network with other professionals and stay up-to-date with industry trends.

3. Work with a team - Surround yourself with a team of professionals, including a manager, publicist, and agent, who can help you stay informed and keep up with industry changes.

Section 2: Career Longevity and Legacy Building as a Hip Hop Artist

Creating a legacy as a hip hop artist requires more than just releasing hit songs and performing at concerts. It involves building a brand identity that resonates with your fans, creating an image and style that stand the test of time, and consistently producing quality music and content.

To achieve career longevity and sustainability, you may need to diversify your revenue streams, such as through merchandise sales, endorsements, and collaborations with other brands and artists. You can also explore new markets and audiences, such as through international tours and collaborations with artists from other regions.

Building a long-lasting career and leaving a positive legacy is essential for any hip hop artist. Here are some key steps to follow:

1. Stay true to yourself - Authenticity is important to building a long-lasting career. Focus on developing your unique style and approach to music.

2. Continuously grow and evolve -

Continuously push yourself to grow and evolve as an artist. Experiment with new sounds and styles, collaborate with other artists, and stay open to feedback.

3. Build a strong brand - Develop a strong brand that reflects your music and style. Consistency is key to building a strong brand.

4. Leave a positive legacy - Use your platform to make a positive impact on the world. Support important causes, inspire your fans, and leave a legacy that you can be proud of.

Section 3: Giving Back and Mentoring the Next Generation of Music Artists

As a successful music artist, it's important to give back to your community and help mentor and support the next generation of artists. This may involve volunteering at local music programs, hosting workshops and seminars for young artists, or providing financial support and resources to aspiring musicians.

Giving back can help you to build strong relationships within your community and maintain a positive reputation as a music artist. It can also inspire and motivate the next generation of artists to follow in your footsteps and achieve their dreams.

Giving back and mentoring the next generation of music artists is an important part of being a hip hop artist. Here are some key steps to follow:

1. Mentor young artists - Share your knowledge and experience with young

artists who are just starting out. Offer advice and feedback on their music and career development.

2. Collaborate with up-and-coming artists - Collaborate with up-and-coming artists to provide an opportunity for them to gain exposure and experience.

3. Give back to your community - Use your platform to give back to your community. Support local charities and initiatives that are important to you.

4. Be a positive role model - Use your celebrity status to be a positive role model for young people. Lead by example and inspire others to achieve their dreams.

Staying ahead of the game is crucial to maintaining a successful and long-lasting career as a hip hop artist. By keeping up with industry trends and changes, building a strong brand and leaving a positive legacy, and giving back and mentoring the next generation of music artists, you can achieve your goals, make a positive impact on the world, and leave a lasting legacy as a respected and admired artist. By adopting a proactive approach to your career, staying informed and adaptable, and creating a positive impact within your community, you can achieve long-term success and inspire future generations of music artists. Remember that your career is more than just making music; it's about creating a legacy and leaving a lasting impact on the music industry and your community.

CHAPTER 7

Crafting Your Sound and Style

Crafting your sound and style is a crucial aspect of becoming a successful hip hop artist. It involves finding your unique voice and creating a sound that sets you apart from other artists in the crowded music industry. It is all about telling your story, bringing your distinctive perspective and style to the forefront, and engaging your audience with your musical persona.

One of the first steps in crafting your sound and style is studying the greats. It is important to understand the history and evolution of hip hop, part of which includes paying homage to the pioneers and legends of the genre. This helps musicians learn the foundational techniques as well as the unwritten nuances of the craft.

Another key aspect of crafting your sound and style is experimenting with different musical styles. By exploring different sounds and musical genres, you can broaden your palette and incorporate diverse elements into your hip hop music. One way to expand your repertoire is by collaborating with musicians from different genres or who bring different styles into your production.

Authenticity is critical to creating a successful album or show. Audiences can recognize a lack of sincerity in the voice, the lyrics, or the demeanor of an artist. To stay authentic, it is important to stay true to your values and beliefs. In today's music industry, it can be tempting to compromise on artistic integrity in favor of commercial success, but this approach can ultimately hinder your integrity as an artist.

Finally, another critical aspect of crafting your sound and style is staying true to your artistic vision. Surround yourself with people who support your ambitions, who you trust and who will positively influence your sound and style. It is always good to have a team of professionals who can bring new ideas and perspectives to the table.

Section 1: Finding Your Unique Voice and Sound as a Hip Hop Artist

Finding your unique voice and sound is key to standing out as a hip hop artist. Here are some key steps to follow:

1. Study the greats - Study the pioneers and legends of hip hop to learn the history and evolution of the genre.

2. Experiment with different styles - Experiment with different styles of hip hop, including boom bap, trap, and alternative hip hop.

3. Define your message - Determine the message that you want to convey through your music. What are you passionate about? What are your experiences and perspectives?

4. Be true to yourself - Stay true to yourself and your story. Don't try to imitate other artists, but instead, focus on developing your own unique voice and style.

Section 2: Exploring Different Musical Styles and Influences

Exploring different musical styles and

influences is essential to creating a fresh and innovative sound as a hip hop artist. Here are some key steps to follow:

1. Listen to different genres - Listen to different genres of music, such as jazz, soul, funk, and rock, to broaden your musical palette and incorporate different elements into your hip hop sound.

2. Collaborate with diverse artists - Collaborate with artists from different musical backgrounds and genres to learn new techniques and make exciting music.

3. Travel and immerse yourself in different cultures - Travel to different parts of the world and immerse yourself in different cultures to gain new perspectives and incorporate global sounds into your music.

Section 3: Tips for Staying Authentic and True to Yourself

Staying authentic and true to yourself is important to building a loyal fan base and staying true to your artistic vision. Here are some key tips to follow:

1. Be honest in your lyrics - Use your lyrics to express your thoughts, feelings, and experiences honestly.

2. Stay true to your values - Stay true to your values and beliefs in your music and in your public persona.

3. Don't compromise for success - Don't compromise your artistic vision or integrity for commercial success.

4. Surround yourself with a supportive

team - Surround yourself with a team of professionals who share your vision and can support you in staying true to yourself.

The process of crafting one's sound and style as an artist is ongoing, and takes time and dedication to establish. It requires musicians to understand the foundations of the genre, be open to collaboration, maintain artistic integrity, and stay true to themselves while ensuring they are keeping pace with the ever-evolving industry. By doing so, musicians can create a unique sound that sets them apart and resonates with their audience, leading to long-term success in their career.

CHAPTER 8

*Creating and Releasing
Your Music*

Creating and recording music can be a long and challenging process, but it is also incredibly rewarding. The ability to express yourself through music and create something that resonates with others can be a powerful experience. In this chapter, we will explore the process of creating and recording music, as well as strategies for releasing and promoting your music to the world.

The Process of Creating and Recording Music

The first step in creating your music is coming up with a song or an idea. This can be anything from a catchy melody to a set of lyrics that speak to you. Once you have your idea, the next step is to start building the song. This can involve experimenting with different chord progressions, melodies or beats.

When it comes to recording, there are many options available to you. You can record at home using a computer and a microphone, or you can book studio time for a more polished sound. It is essential to take the time to get the best quality recordings possible. This means investing in high-quality equipment, whether that is a microphone or a mixing console.

Mixing is an essential part of the recording process, as it involves balancing the different elements of the track to create a cohesive and polished sound. Mixing is where the recording comes to life and can make or break the song. It is important to take the time to get the mix right, either by doing it yourself or hiring a professional mix engineer.

Strategies for Releasing Your Music

Once your music is mixed and ready to go, it is time to release it to the world. One key aspect of releasing your music is choosing the right release date. This can involve researching other releases that are coming out around the same time and choosing a date that doesn't clash with other significant releases.

Marketing your music is also an essential strategy for getting your music out there. This can involve creating social media campaigns, releasing sneak peeks of the music, or partnering with other artists to create a buzz. It is important to leverage your existing fan base and build on that as you promote your music.

Getting Your Music on Streaming Services and Gaining Exposure

Finally, the step is to get your music on streaming services like Spotify, Apple Music, or Tidal. This involves working with a distributor who can get your music onto these platforms. It is also essential to take advantage of all the tools on these streaming services, such as playlists and editorial sections.

Gaining exposure is another crucial aspect of releasing your music. One way to do this is to perform live shows and get booked at music festivals. Collaboration with other artists can also help you gain exposure and attract a wider audience. Pitching your music to blogs and music publications can also be an effective way to get your music out there.

Creating and releasing music can be a long and challenging process. However, by taking the time to get the recording and mixing right, selecting the right release date, and marketing your music using different strategies, you can create an excellent debut that will resonate with your audience.

CHAPTER 9

Touring and Live Performance

Touring and live performance are essential aspects of being a successful hip hop artist. Performing in front of a live audience can be a transformative experience, allowing artists to connect with their fans and build a loyal fan base. In this chapter, we will explore preparing for live performances and touring, engaging with your audience, and strategies for marketing and promoting your live shows.

Preparing for Live Performances and Touring

Preparing for a live performance involves much more than just learning the lyrics and rehearsing the songs. It is essential to work out the logistics, such as transportation and accommodation, and to ensure you have all the necessary equipment and gear. It is also important to rehearse the performance itself, including choreography, stage presence, and interacting with the audience.

Touring involves taking this preparation to the next level, as it means performing in front of multiple audiences over an extended period. Again, it is important to have a solid plan in place, including booking the right venues and planning the travel schedule. It is essential to maintain a strong work ethic and discipline on tour.

Engaging with Your Audience and Building Your Fanbase

Engaging with your audience is a crucial part of live performance. Rap music is, by nature, an interactive medium that relies on the energy and engagement of the audience. Artists can engage with their audience in many ways, from encouraging audience response during a song to breaking down the lyrics and storytelling. Interacting with your audience can help to build a loyal fan base, which is essential to the success of a hip hop artist.

Building a fan base is not just about performing live shows; it is also about staying connected with your fans in between shows. Social media platforms such as Instagram, Twitter and Facebook can be incredibly useful for engaging with fans, keeping them informed about new music releases or upcoming shows.

Strategies for Marketing and Promoting Your Live Shows

Marketing and promoting your live shows is a critical aspect of the touring process. There are many ways to market your shows, such as creating social media campaigns or using paid advertising, such as Facebook ads. It is also beneficial to work with local promoters or venues to help spread the word about your upcoming show.

Working with merchandising companies to produce merchandise can also be an effective way to promote live shows. Fans are often eager to buy merchandise like T-shirts or hoodies, which can help to create buzz and create more interest in your live performances.

In conclusion, touring and live performance can be challenging, but also incredibly rewarding for hip hop artists. Preparing for live performances and touring, engaging with your audience and building your fan base, and developing strategies for marketing and promoting your live shows can help to take your career to the next level. By mastering these skills, you can create a loyal following and connect with fans in a meaningful way.

CHAPTER 10

The Future of Hip Hop

Hip hop has evolved significantly over the years and has become one of the most globally popular genres. In this final chapter, we will examine the current state of hip hop and explore where the genre is headed, identify emerging trends and opportunities in the music industry, and discuss how hip hop artists can stay ahead of the curve.

Examining the Current State of Hip Hop and Where the Genre is Headed

Hip hop has seen enormous growth and success in recent years, with more artists from diverse backgrounds emerging in the genre. The popularity of hip hop has allowed it to embrace different sub-genres and styles, such as trap, drill, and Afrobeat.

The genre's future is expected to be shaped by emerging trends and catalysts, such as social media platforms and changing music distribution models. Industry insiders predict that hip hop's evolution will be driven by several factors, including experimentation with new sounds and adoption by mainstream audiences.

Identifying Emerging Trends and Opportunities in the Music Industry

Emerging trends and opportunities in the music industry are creating new pathways for hip hop artists. One of the most significant opportunities is the growth of streaming services like Spotify and Apple Music, which offer artists the chance to reach a global audience.

Other opportunities include collaborations with brands and companies to promote their products, as well as the ability to leverage social media platforms to connect with fans and promote music.

Staying Ahead of the Curve and Continuously Evolving as a Hip Hop Artist

Hip hop artists must stay ahead of the curve by continuously evolving their sound, style and staying relevant to new audiences. The ability to experiment with new sounds and styles, work with other artists, and adapt to the ever-changing industry landscape is critical to staying ahead of the curve.

Moreover, hip hop artists need to leverage technology and social media platforms to grow their brand and connect with fans. Staying informed about industry trends, new technologies and working with experienced professionals can all help hip hop artists to stay ahead of the curve.

The future of hip hop is promising, and the genre is expected to continue evolving, embracing new styles and sounds. Identifying emerging trends and opportunities in the music industry, and staying ahead of the curve will be critical for hip hop artists who wish to succeed in the long term. By continuously evolving and staying relevant, hip hop artists can create a lasting legacy in the genre that resonates with fans around the world.